BEING ALIVE IS A GOOD IDEA:

A Wide-Ranging Conversation with Nikki Giovanni & Glory Edim

Copyright © 2021 by Independent Bookstore Day Publishing
First (and only) Edition
Printed in the United States of America for Independent Bookstore Day

Series editor: Samantha Schoech
Book designer: Melissa Napolitano
ISBN 9781732970465

All rights reserved. No part of this book may be reproduced, scanned, or distributed in any form without permission.

Independent Bookstore Day Publishing
A program of the American Booksellers Association
www.indiebookstoreday.com

ACKNOWLEDGMENTS

Independent Bookstore Day would like to thank Nikki Giovanni and Glory Edim for their support of readers and bookstores.

INTRODUCTION

The first poems I ever loved were written by Nikki Giovanni. I read the poem "Ego Tripping (there may be a reason why)" non-stop in the eighth grade. Unlike anything I'd read before, the poem celebrated the world of Blackness, all of the beauty we'd been a part of throughout history. She refers to the Congo, journeys to the pyramids, and in the sixth stanza, Giovanni writes, "I turned myself into myself." The entire poem is an exhilarating experience. It's a poem that every Black child should read, and it is timeless in the way that some of Langston Hughes' poems are. The rhythm is infectious and the sentiments undeniably affirming. At thirteen, I found it absolutely mesmerizing. It made me feel immensely proud of my African heritage. I debated reciting the poem for our middle school talent show, but ended up joining a dance group with my two best friends, Ida and Selma, instead—awkwardly gyrating to LL Cool J's 1996 single "*Doin It.*"

I wouldn't hear Giovanni's magnificent voice reciting poetry until I entered college. In 1971, she recorded *Truth Is on Its Way* with the New York Community Choir at Alice Tully Hall in Lincoln Center. The soaring choir and powerful piano chords somehow bolstered the plain-spoken beauty of her poetry. My favorite childhood poem—"Ego Tripping"—was brought to life over and over again. That became an award-winning album that sold 100,000 copies in its first six months. The idea of weaving soulful poetry with traditional Black gospel was out-the-box in 1971.

Years later, in my college dorm room, it remained a marvelous, awe-inspiring combination. Giovanni presented all the sides of Black life, the good, the bad, and the ugly, as well as the beauty, resilience, and joy of her experience, with such fierce honesty that there was no way you couldn't listen. "Peace, be still," sings the choir. The album is a beautiful, joyful, raucous celebration of Black history, ending with some of the most stunning lines in Giovanni's oeuvre:

"*I am so perfect so divine so ethereal so surreal,*
I cannot be comprehended,
except by my permission."

I listened to the album whenever I felt uncertain about my future. When I changed college majors—from history to sociology, and finally to journalism—when I missed my father, when I needed a significant boost to my self-esteem: the record was there. Giovanni's voice was a constant reminder of who I aspired to be in the world—a Black woman who moved through the world, eloquent, audacious, and self-assured.

Truth Is on Its Way is Nikki's musical masterpiece. I danced alone countless times in my dorm, bumping my hips into my twin bed. It unexpectedly became the soundtrack of my college experience. I would invite my friends over to close their eyes and listen. Together we recited Nikki's lyrics, read James Baldwin, and studied the Black Arts Movement.

There is little doubt that a remarkable cultural revolution was born in 1965, and Giovanni was in the center of it all. She emerged as an unconventional leader of this period—a Black woman whose boldness would nurture generations of Black readers. In 1971, James Baldwin and Nikki Giovanni taped a two-hour "dialogue" for a public TV show called *Soul!* At forty-seven years old, Baldwin was already a legend for *The Fire Next Time* and countless other essays, novels, and criticism. Giovanni was only twenty-eight at the time, yet she was charismatic, outspoken, and fearless throughout the interview. The two of them discussed Black manhood, white racism, the role of the writer, and the responsibility to teach. Across generations, the two intellectuals hashed out political and artistic philosophies, which sometimes diverged.

Nikki Giovanni was an unapologetic force. By the time I entered Howard University, I was desperate to embody her nature. But how do you become a poem?

Giovanni has undeniably influenced an entire generation of Black writers. I am not an anomaly. Her presence at the 2020 Well-Read Black Girl Virtual Festival left the audience riveted and full of wonder. We watched her closely from our laptops, taking note of how to live a full, abundant life. Whether you are reading her powerful work or listening to one of her many humorous stories, Giovanni is encouraging us to embrace the complications of Black culture, politics, pop culture, and everything in between. She reminds us that telling our stories out loud is a necessity; the very act strengthens community, and in many cases, it is a matter of survival. Giovanni's voice is also tender, filled with constant laughter and fond memories. Her abiding love for Black people is steadfast and encouraging. When she smiles her one-of-a-kind smile, I am suddenly a freshman in college again, writing in the margins of her beloved books. I'm reciting the last stanza of "Ego Tripping" to myself:

"*I mean . . . I . . . can fly*
like a bird in the sky . . ."

This is the unyielding power of her wildly ambitious legacy. Nikki Giovanni's words make you believe in life's possibilities. *She invites you to take flight!* This transcribed conversation holds her signature wit, compassion, and vivid storytelling that will always leave us enamored. She removes the fear and leaves us with so much more. She tells us "being alive is a good idea." We can't help but agree.

Glory Edim
Founder of Well-Read Black Girl
February 2021

- -

Make Me Rain

make me rain
turn me into a snowflake

let me rest
on your tongue

make me a piece of ice
so I can cool you

let me be the cloud
that embraces you

or the quilt
that get you dry

snuggle close
listen to me sing

on the windowsill

make me rain
on you

Copyright © 1968 by Nikki Giovanni. Used with permission of the author.

Nikki Giovanni: I really like that poem.

I've been doing a lot with water. *Make Me Rain*[1] is my latest book, but the book just before that was *A Good Cry*.[2] And so I've been doing a lot with water because, you know, you can go a long time without eating, but you can't go very long without water. And I think that we have to have a little more respect for water.

I'm sure we all know Joy Reid[3]. I've been invited on the show. Now Biden has been elected, which I couldn't be happier about, and we've got Kamala Harris as vice president, so I don't know that I will actually get on, but they always ask you things like, "What would you do if you were president?" There are two things I would do right away. I would outlaw golf courses. Just get rid of them. I mean, where are the chipmunks going to live? Where are the squirrels going to live? How are the little deer going to get along? Just so some fool like Donald Trump can sit there and lie about his score? I think that the point of golf courses is to prevent other people from being part of it because golf clubs are expensive.

The other thing that I would do—if anybody's listening to poets—is not allow any building to be over sixty feet tall. You have to realize, we urinate, among other things, in water. There are people on Earth who don't have water to drink. So, can you imagine: You have a building that's a hundred and twenty stories high. Look how much water, right? That water has to pump all the way up, you urinate, and it has to pump all the way back down to be cleaned. That has to stop and so I think

---

[1] *Make Me Rain: Poems and Prose*, 2020 (William Morrow)

[2] *A Good Cry: What We Learn for Tears and Laughter*, 2017 (HarperCollins)

[3] Joy-Ann M. Lomena-Reid, known professionally as Joy Reid, is an American cable television host and political commentator. She hosts *The ReidOut* show on MSNBC.

that if I get to talk with Joy, I'm hoping she'll ask that so I'll get to say get rid of golf courses and get rid of tall buildings.

Glory Edim: We can make a petition for you to be on Joy Reid's show. We will support that 100%.

Thank you so much for being with us today. You need no introduction in this community. We are more than fans, we are lifelong lovers of your work. I have all the books that you've been in here. I have Marie Evans[4]. I have Tony Cade Bambara's *The Black Woman*—the first time I really fully understood *Rosa*[5] was when I was reading this book right here. Of course, I have your newest book, which is phenomenal. You know, I love the poem "Big Sisters."[6] There's so many beautiful poems in here.

You have given us so much hope. You taught us how to love through poetry. You affirmed us, made us feel beautiful and seen. You've helped us discover our political ideologies. The first time I read a poem by you I knew I could be angry. I knew I could cuss a motherfucker out. It all came from you. There was a poet who said those beautiful words: "radical sustainability." You have been radical in your work and you've been able to sustain it and have a life that is beautiful and worthy of admiration. All that to say that we bow at your feet.

Giovanni: Ha. Thank you. You know, I'm still teaching—I guess I'll teach until they fire me or I drop dead in the classroom—but I'm always reminding my students, don't be afraid to contradict yourself. I was listening to some of the younger women—I'm 77—I think that the main

---

[4] *Black Women Writers, 1950-1980*

[5] "Nikki-Rosa" from *Black Feeling, Black Talk, Black Judgement* by Nikki Giovanni, 1968, 1970.

[6] "Big Sisters" from *Make Me Rain*, 2020

thing as you're writing is that you are not afraid of contradicting yourself, that you don't mind being where you are today. And if you do that, you'll allow yourself to grow. You don't write for other people, you write for yourself. You are your first audience. You're the person that has to say, "Oh, that makes sense that I've learned something." Then you move on. I think that's so important.

Big Sisters

Big Sisters:
have dimples
can sing
play the piano
tap-dance
read books
talk on the phone
paint their toenails
overnight with friends

while

Little Sisters
look on
and
love

Copyright ©2020 by Nikki Giovanni. Used with permission of the author.

Edim: How do you put the contradiction into practice? When you're writing at nineteen, you're saying these things and then you look back at fifty, or even twenty-five. Like, what does that look like on a daily basis?

Giovanni: It was kind of interesting to listen to some of my older poems. One of the poems that I think we all love is "Ego Tripping."[7] I mean, I love that. And I love "Nikki-Rosa," and I love some other poems. But I wouldn't write "Nigger can you kill"[8] anymore because we've moved beyond that. In this book, I'm very proud that I have some poems for Black Lives Matter because Black women have been so important to changes on Earth, particularly in America.

It was so nice to hear Vice President Harris give her speech last night[9] saying how proud she is of Black women and naming those whose shoulders she stands on. The only person she missed was Fannie Lou Hamer[10]. She would not have been there if Fannie Lou Hamer had not created the Mississippi Freedom Democratic Party. You know how poor Black people in Mississippi were. Well, they saved their money, rented a bus, and went to the 1964 Democratic Convention and demanded to be seated. Lyndon Johnson finally realized he had a problem. Lyndon Johnson was a great politician, that's reality, and so he came to Mrs. Hamer and he said,

---

[7] "Ego Tripping (there may be a reason why)" by Nikki Giovanni, 1968

[8] From "My Poem," Nikki Giovanni, 1968

[9] This conversation took place the day after Harris and Biden made their victory speeches on November 7, 2020.

[10] Fannie Lou Hamer (1917–1977) was an American voting and women's rights activist, community organizer, and a leader in the civil rights movement. She was the co-founder and vice-chair of the Freedom Democratic Party, which she represented at the 1964 Democratic National Convention. Hamer also organized Mississippi's Freedom Summer along with the Student Nonviolent Coordinating Committee (SNCC), and was a co-founder of the National Women's Political Caucus, an organization created to recruit, train, and support women of all races who wished to seek election to government office.

"Well, let's see if we can work this out. Why don't we give you two seats of the four and in the next four years we'll have worked it out." Fannie Lou Hamer looked at him and said, "We didn't come here for no two seats." I have always remembered that. It just really touches me.

After, she and her group, the Mississippi Freedom Democratic Party, got on the bus and went back to Mississippi. Well, the minute that that bus crossed the Mississippi state line the sheriff and his people—and they're all cowards because they always do everything together—took her off the bus and they beat her. And I always said, no matter what—I'm not good at biology, but I think it's your liver that's the last thing that stops—I've always said if there's nothing left but my liver take my liver to the polling place and remember Mrs. Hamer and vote because it meant that much to her. I will never not vote. Somebody can say, "Well, I don't like this and I don't like that." Nobody gives a damn what you like. We're talking about what people have gone through so that you can stand in line. And when I looked at the people in Atlanta and I looked at the people in Detroit, I was so proud of Black people. It is not a question of what you like. It was two men running against each other, just that one is evil in one isn't. Trump is evil. If Hitler had married Satan, Trump would be their son. But Black people were saying very clearly that we have a voice and it will be heard.

The only thing that Vice President Harris missed, and that's easy enough because a lot of people don't know Mrs. Hamer or don't realize the importance of what she's done. She remembered the people that she remembered, like Mrs. Chisholm[11], which is normal because her parents

---

[11] Shirley Anita Chisholm (1924 – 2005) was a politician, educator, and author. In 1968, she became the first Black woman elected to the United States Congress, representing New York's 12th congressional district for seven terms from 1969 to 1983.

are also immigrants. I knew Shirley—we didn't hang out, but I knew Shirley Chisholm. But I will always—until my liver stops, until there's nothing on me—I will always remember Mrs. Hamer, and I will always remember the beating that she took so that I could vote. And I will always vote.

Nikki-Rosa

childhood remembrances are always a drag
if you're Black
you always remember things like living in Woodlawn
with no inside toilet
and if you become famous or something
they never talk about how happy you were to have
your mother
all to yourself and
how good the water felt when you got your bath
from one of those
big tubs that folk in chicago barbecue in
and somehow when you talk about home
it never gets across how much you
understood their feelings
as the whole family attended meetings about Hollydale
and even though you remember
your biographers never understand
your father's pain as he sells his stock
and another dream goes
And though you're poor it isn't poverty that
concerns you

and though they fought a lot
it isn't your father's drinking that makes any difference
but only that everybody is together and you
and your sister have happy birthdays and very good
Christmases
and I really hope no white person ever has cause
to write about me
because they never understand
Black love is Black wealth and they'll
probably talk about my hard childhood
and never understand that
all the while I was quite happy

Copyright © 1968, 1970 by Nikki Giovanni. Used with permission of the author.

Edim: We are beyond grateful for their legacy and for their ability to show us what can happen when you demand. As you said, she went there and she didn't say, "Can you please do this for me?" She demanded the seats. She wanted to be in the space and she didn't allow people to minimize her in any way, and I think that is a lesson that we hold dear. We have to demand what is ours and what we need to have in this society. And now that we have this VP—it's not the only thing that needs to change, but it is a step in the right direction. So what was your reaction—because I know we were flipping out over here—when you found out the news [about the 2020 presidential election]?

Giovanni: I never had any question Biden was going to win. It never occurred to me. I grew up in the Baptist Church with my grandmother and my mother was AME, African Methodist Episcopal. I have friends and they were saying, "Oh, we're worried Trump's going to find a way." I said, no. God has shown us, get off your butts and do something, and we did. I mean, God was on that. He said, "I don't care if it's raining or snowing. I don't care. You get out there and you vote." And we did. I never had any question, as I don't have any question that, as Vice President Harris was saying, "I am the first"—which she is—"but I won't be the last." That's quite true. We will have a Black woman be president of the United States. If I was betting, I will never bet that it will be Ms. Harris. She will have done what she was supposed to do. It will be one of these youngsters, one of you kids will be the ones that will do. Because otherwise your ambition—I'm not ambitious; that's one of my problems—but you have to make sure that your ambition doesn't get in the way of your responsibility and your duty.

Edim: Mm hm. The other day we put something on our Instagram talking about the idea of power and how when you get a little bit of power, you need to be able to be on the side of human justice. What are your thoughts about—I was going to try to say it nice—but these crazies, Ice Cube[12] and Lil Wayne[13] and all these people who were defending Donald Trump? They have power, they have access and money, and they're Black men saying this. What do we do when we're faced with people that are just not in support of the community?

---

[12] Ice Cube is a rapper, actor, and filmmaker. His lyrics on N.W.A's 1988 album *Straight Outta Compton* contributed to gangsta rap's widespread popularity. In 2020, he angered fans by working with Donald Trump on the "Contract with Black America."

[13] Lil Wayne is a rapper, singer, songwriter, record executive, entrepreneur, and actor. He is regarded by many contemporaries as one of the most influential hip hop artists of his generation, and often cited as one of the greatest rappers of all time. He endorsed President Trump during the election campaign, praising his work on criminal reform. Lil Wayne was pardoned by Trump for a weapons charge on his last day in office.

Giovanni: Well, I think they need to be hospitalized. We know that they are obviously crazy. We know that Kanye West is crazy. We know that he has sold not just Black people out, he has sold out America. He'd sold out the world. I saw that Ice Cube was, "Well, I was just going to—." I said, 'Nah." Cube was wrong and there's no way to stop that. I don't buy Ice Cube. I'm not going to be one of the ten thousand people jumping up and down going to him. I have said it before, but I really like the direction that young women like Beyoncé are going. She is doing something to help people. I love the way that athletes are going and it is very disappointing to see the so-called rappers. One of the most important young men *ever* in our community, Tupac—

Edim: I know you have your tattoo.[14] And that's it. You have the opportunity to make such a great difference with your platform and then you choose to do something like that. It is just so baffling to me and I always wonder what Tupac would have become if he had the opportunity to grow into full adulthood and continue the work that he was doing. Who knows what his legacy would have been and what he would have said about this election.

Giovanni: We do know. One of the reasons that he's not here is that everybody figured if 'Pac is here, he will make a difference. 'Pac is one of the people who were shot like Martin Luther King was shot. Am I making sense? They wanted to get rid of him so that you would end up with sons of bitches like Ice Cube and them who they can buy. They're like slaves. Somebody like a Donald Trump comes along and says, "I will give you this."

That's being a Judas. It is. I think that our community needs to recognize

---

[14] Giovanni has a "Thug Life" tattoo on the inside of her forearm.

it, which I think we do, and I think that our community has every right to be upset and to turn our backs on them. And I do say they're a Judas because Judas was trying to explain, "Well, I needed a job. I just needed some money." You got to be crazy. Judas was wrong, but so was Simon. Simon was like, "I'm with you, don't worry, Judas." And then when they came, what did he say? He said, "I don't know him." We've seen all of this. Who did we have at the cross? We had his mother. And we who are mothers are always going to be there. As sad as that must be to sit there and watch your son's blood drop. But we had his mother and we had the disciple John the Beloved and the rest of those people. Jesus knew what he was doing when he said to John, "Take care of my mother." He knew the rest of them people were no good. He always knew that.

Edim: One-hundred percent. We [WRBG] are an intergenerational community and we work with an incredible organization called The Sadie Nash Leadership Project,[15] and they have submitted a wonderful question from a young student. In your poem "Vote,"[16] you speak about the importance of everyone having access to voting and exercising their right as citizens. Sadie Nash focuses on supporting young women and gender non-conforming young people to grow as leaders in their communities and beyond. What message do you have for young people who are exercising and claiming the right to participate in our democracy right now about the future of voting and the future of politics in the U.S.?

Giovanni: I think we all just do the best we can. Everybody is not going to be a leader. You hear that all the time, "Well, I think I should be a leader." But somebody has to follow and I think that's important. I have a

---

[15] www.sadienash.org

[16] The poem "Vote" appears in *Make Me Rain*, 2020 (Wiliam Morrow)

poem that I love a lot, too, and the poem says, "But some of us stayed."[17] I mean, who's not proud of Harriet Tubman? How could you not be? Who's not proud of Frederick Douglass? I said to my class the other day, "If I had lived during Douglass's time, I would have screwed him. It would have been a great thing."

Edim: I used to have the biggest crush on Frederick Douglass and people would be like, "Fredrick Douglass?" and I'm like, "Nah, Frederick Douglass could *get* it."

Giovanni: Yeah! But, some of us stayed and that's what I wanted to deal with and that's what that poem deals with. Some people ran, some people could talk, but some of us stayed and we built communities, we built churches. There's a poet named Kwame Dawes[18] and he talks about how some of us had to cut our sons down from trees and wipe the sick off of them. We had to comfort our daughters after they had been raped by those white cowards, and we still stayed. We said this is our country and we had made a promise to our people. We're going to stay. We will be here for you. And I was very glad to hear—and we'll see how it works out—that last night Biden said, "When I started this, you had my back." He was clear. You didn't have to wonder what he meant because he was clear. Then he said, "And I want you to know, I'm going to have yours." Black lives *matter* and if we can make sure that something like the president of the United States knows that Black lives matter, then we're going to be able to show the cowards—because they're cowards. And they will go away.

---

[17] "But Some of Us Stayed," from *Make Me Rain*.

[18] Kwame Dawes is the author of twenty books of poetry and numerous other books of fiction, criticism, and essays.

Like in 1946, for example, in Germany, once the Nazis were defeated, all of a sudden nobody was a Nazi. Everybody's like "*I* wasn't a Nazi!" We were talking about Peter and all of the disciples? "*I* wasn't a disciple." All of a sudden they went away, and these cowards are going to go away also. I hate the term "white supremacy." It's not a term that I use because there's nothing supreme about what they are. They are white cowards, and it's time that we called—as Aretha said, "Let's call this game exactly what it is."

Edim: You are dropping so many gems for us. I'm going back to the question box, and this is a great question given quarantine. We were just talking about your virtual tour for your new book because everything's been online. Has this time of stillness and isolation impacted your writing and creative process? How has it been to be alone during this time?

Giovanni: Well, writers are always alone. Writers and painters. I think we're used to being alone. And I'm also an Appalachian because I was born in Knoxville, Tennessee, and I grew up in Cincinnati and I am now here at Virginia Tech, back in Appalachia. So I'm used to being alone. I think it's the city kids—I'm not picking on them—but the city kids live close to each other, they're used to noise. We're in the country here. You heard my dog, but it's quiet. So I'm used to quiet. And I'm a space freak and I talk about space a lot—I talk about space a lot, period—but I talk about it a lot in *Make Me Rain*. When we look at who went to space when the United States and Russia were having their space war, who do we look to? We look to the people from Appalachia. We look for John Glenn. We look to the people who spent so much time alone that going into space was not unusual.

Now we know—and I talked about that a lot and I wish I could do more with it—that as we begin to understand our galaxy—and we live in a great galaxy; I think it's just fabulous—we know that the best person to go into space is the Black woman because she can get along with everyone. No matter what else is going on, Black women get along. If somebody says, "Well, the aliens might bother you," I say, "Don't tell me about the aliens. I've been living with aliens for 200 years." It's the truth. We came here. You think these weren't aliens? You think Donald Trump's not an alien? Of course they are. So, if we're gonna go meet our other living life forms in the galaxy, the Black woman is going to have to be the one that leads that.

Edim: Yes. Let's do it. Let's get back into space. There are many mothers and educators that are on our feed and they want to know what ideas we should share with the children in our lives to help them understand race and Black pride and liberty. What do you hope or imagine for the future of young people?

Giovanni: Well, again, I'm not namby-pamby, but I think that it's very important that everybody—and, again, Black women are going to have to lead this—understand that we live on the third planet from the yellow sun and we need to learn to refer to ourselves as Earthlings. As long as we keep trying to use race or countries—for example, if right now a life form came and said, you know, "Hi, who are you and where am I?" I couldn't possibly say I am living in Virginia because it wouldn't make any sense. I would have to say I live on the third planet from the yellow sun. I am an Earthling.

I think we as Black mothers—and we are *Black*—but there's no such thing as race because we're all the same race. I think that's one of the things we need to move away from, trying to pretend that we're Swedish or German or Russian. All of that is so old. I think that Black women are going to be the people who lead that and I think it's important that we do.

Now, somebody will write in and say, "Well, I think it's important to be Black." Well, you *are* Black. Nobody can take that away. Nobody is trying to. What we're trying to do is make sure that our children understand that we are on a planet and that planet belongs to all of us and we have to learn not just to get along and be friendly—none of that little crap—but to understand that we are Earthlings. Now, everybody on Earth sings our music—we were talking about rap—but from the spirituals to jazz to rhythm and blues. Everybody hears our music just like everybody eats Chinese food. I ask my students, "Who here has had Chinese food?" and all of their hands go up. That's good. "How many of you speak Chinese?" One person can speak Chinese. I said, "Don't you think that one of the things we should be doing now is making sure that we learn how other people speak, the languages they speak?" And, of course, Joe Biden is married to a teacher, to Jill, and he was saying, "We have to pay some more attention to the teachers." We do. But we need to be hiring some Chinese teachers. We need to be hiring everyone. If you picked up your phone right now and called anything, they would say, "Press one for English, press two for Spanish." I think it's time that we extend it. And, again, I count on Black women because we are not afraid. Black women are not cowards. We have stood up against everything and we have stood up against everything not only with joy, but with love. We have done a wonderful, wonderful job. And so I think that Black women are going to have to continue to stand up for the future, for that which is better.

Edim: I'm just…I feel so full from everything you're saying because it literally is what we've been talking about all weekend—knowing your self-worth, being able to set boundaries and understand your agency. It's so important to be self-reflective and introspective when it comes to these ideas and learning how to put them into practice because it's not enough to just say it or share it in a tweet. You really need to embody it in your everyday life.

Right now there are so many folks that are going back and watching your videos from the '70s and '80s and they're so excited to read and learn your work and to revisit it. Everything's going viral. The video with you and James Baldwin[19] is a classic. Everyone refers to that video, with good reason, but why do you think it feels even more precious and significant right now?

Giovanni: I was amazed when people started to talk to me about that because, as I say, I don't really do my old work. I don't read it. People say, "Oh, that that conversation with James Baldwin." And I say, "How did you hear that?" And so I finally realized, okay, I guess it's gone viral.

I'm not allowed to touch machines. Ginney[20] sets everything up and then I can come and talk to you and then I have to just sit there until it dies or whatever it is that it does. I have learned how to—what is that thing?—text. I know how to text. I'm trying to learn how to send photos. My son lives in New York and I want to send photos because we both cook. He's a very good cook. I'm a very good cook. And so we laugh about what I'm cooking, and we want to send photos back and forth. And I have

---

[19] In 1971, Nikki Giovanni and James Baldwin appeared in conversation together on PBS's *SOUL!* Baldwin was forty-six at the time; Giovanni was twenty-eight. The transcript was published as *A Dialogue* (1973) with a preface by Ida Lewis. The video is available on YouTube.

[20] Virginia Fowler is a professor of English at Virginia Tech, where she directs undergraduate studies in English. She teaches courses in African American literature, in women writers, and in the fiction of Toni Morrison. She is currently an associate producer of the forthcoming documentary *Going to Mars: The Nikki Giovanni Project.*

a dear friend—I hope you know his name—Kwame Alexander,[21] and Kwame, he's a great kid. Well, not a kid, I mean, but Kwame and Thomas are within 10 days of each other. So, all three of us cook and we send pictures back and forth. Kwame is cooking meatloaf today, by the way, and I'm making a rack of lamb. We talked last night about it. I may call him back later on and say, "Let me see what it looks like." You know, we laugh, but I am beginning to learn to send photos.

Edim: Well, we can text, we can show you how to text. It's pretty easy.

Giovanni: I say to my students, "You are not allowed to use that word, easy. Because if it's easy, I would have done it." And don't say that to yourself. If it were easy, we wouldn't even be discussing it. Everything is learned at a different time in a different way. Part of being grown, and I am, is to admit, "Well, I haven't learned this but I am working on it." And I think that's fair enough. I think it's fair. So many people think I should know how to do it. And you shouldn't know. What you're doing is admitting, "I'm learning this." I think that's only fair. I think you have to give yourself a break because if you don't then you put pressure on yourself and I'm worried about the kids—and, again, I shouldn't call you kids—but I worry about the young women because I think there's a lot of pressure on you and I think you don't need the pressure. You will do with your life that which comes to you to do and it will come as it comes. So you have to only be—and I say only, but this is not easy either—but you have to listen to yourself. Some things work, some things don't. So give yourself a break and say, "Okay, now is the time for this or now I want to try this, or this didn't work."

---

[21] Kwame Alexander is an American writer of poetry and children's fiction. His verse novel *The Crossover* won the 2015 Newbery Medal recognizing the year's "most distinguished contribution to American literature for children."

I'm a big fan of pencils because pencils have erasers. Everything doesn't work and when it doesn't work, you erase it and go on. I'm a fan of things like divorce. And I'm a big fan of adoption. And if it's one thing that I think is truly unfair, it's youngsters who were adopted and people try to laugh and say, "Oh, your mama didn't want you." That is not true. That's one of the best, biggest acts of love. It's a woman who has carried you next to her heart for nine months, and I don't know if you're a mother, but I can tell you it's uncomfortable. It was a whole lot easier getting it in than getting it out. And then you realize that the best thing you can do for your child is to let them go to another family, to let somebody else help you with them. It's an act of love. And I just get sick of people being so damn stupid because they want to laugh at you. They want to make you feel bad because they're stuck with some fool. Your mother said, "I've done all I can do. I'm going to let you go." That's just not easy.

Edim: If you can say, "I'm going to allow my child to grow up in the best experience and let them go," that's, like, the biggest act of love and kindness there is.

Giovanni: Yeah, I really think it is. I really do.

Edim: I do have a little boy and he is seven months old. I called my friend at BLK MKT Vintage,[22] which is a beautiful online shop that curates Black vintage art and books and clothes. I wanted to have my son hear your album. Here it is [holds up *Nikki Giovanni and the New York Community Choir, Like a Ripple on a Pond*, 1973]. I was like, I need to play this for my son. And so I got this and I have *Truth Is on Its Way*[23] as well.

---

[22] www.blkmktvintage.com

[23] *Truth Is on Its Way* [vinyl album] by Nikki Giovanni and The New York Community Choir, 1970.

So your words are touching my son as well. His name is Zikomo, and I just feel so blessed to be in conversation with you now because you have influenced me so much, in so many ways. You are the reason why WRBG exists. The beauty of your transparency, your openness—I love hearing your stories, too. You're just a great storyteller. Can you tell a story about making this album and how it came together? What was the inspiration behind it? You were so young when you did it as well, but it's iconic.

Giovanni: Yeah. The first one, of course, was *Truth Is on Its Way*. Carl Proctor[24] worked for Columbia Records—I'm not going to keep you here forever—but Columbia signed Aretha Franklin and Carl was her producer. Nobody wanted to listen to Carl and so, ultimately, when that was over, Aretha went to Atlantic Records. So now you have Carl not really knowing what to do. I am always trying to do something different and I love gospel music. Ellis Haizlip[25] owed me favors. That was the opening. That's how I ended up with James Baldwin [on *SOUL!*]. For two years I ended up working with *SOUL!*, the TV show, and I thought, "Well, I really do love spirituals." And I could see how some of my poetry could go with some spirituals. I thought it would be really great to be able to put it together and to do something at Lincoln Center. I was living in New York. Well, of course, I'm a poet. I didn't have any money.

But there was a guy, Patrick McGinnis. Patrick was the manager at Lincoln Center. And so I just called and made an appointment. I said I'd really like to have a program at Lincoln Center and he said this is what we charge and I said, "Oh, Patrick, I don't have any money; I'm a poet."

---

[24] Carl Proctor was the founder of the Right-On record label.

[25] Ellis B. Haizlip (1929 – 1991) was a television and theatrical producer, broadcaster, and promoter of African American culture. Haizlip is best known as the creator, producer, and host of the television variety show *SOUL!*.

He said, "Well, I'm not allowed to just give it away." So I said, "Ok, tell me what you need," and he said, "We could probably do it for about $1,500." And I said, "How many seats is that?" There are 1,500 seats. I believe in the dollar, so I said, "If I could sell out for a dollar a seat it would be all right?" And he said, "You probably won't be able to sell out for a dollar." And I said, "I probably won't, but what will happen to me if I don't?" He said, "Oh, nothing. We'll work it out."

So, I went to work on it. What I needed was a gospel choir. Benny Diggs[26] is up in Harlem and he knew Wilson Pickett and I knew Harold Logan[27]—that's another, longer story—but Harold Logan owned Birdland, so Harold and Pickett were together. I asked Mr. Logan, did he think that Mr. Pickett would mind opening my show. And Wilson Pickett said, yeah, but he wanted Aretha Franklin. I said I can't think of anything that would make me happier than Aretha Franklin—Aretha Franklin and I were friends, we were sorority sisters—but Aretha is serious about business. I mean, she was never going to fool with that. She got paid in *cash*.

So, that wasn't going to work, but Wilson saw what we were doing, came to a couple of rehearsals and said, "I'll be there. I'll do it."

But, of course, what Pickett did as he opened the show—you know, *ladies and gentlemen, please welcome Wilson Pickett*—he came out and he looks around and sings, "I wish Aretha Franklin was here." And I thought, *oh no...* Well, Aretha didn't speak to me for almost two years. I hadn't put him up to it, but she didn't know that.

---

[26] Benny Diggs, a graduate of Harvard, had some success with his own soul group, Revelation, in the 1970s before becoming a songwriter, conductor, producer, and manager.

[27] Harold Logan was a songwriter and club owner who wrote songs for Lloyd Price, Wilson Pickett, and others. He was murdered outside the Turntable in Times Square in 1969 at the age of 45.

We were sold out, by the way, because nobody had seen anything like that and Carl Proctor said, "Why don't we make an album?" And I said, "We just did."

We did not—and Benny and I were laughing about that—we did not make a penny off of this album. That's the truth. It's a dirty business. The music industry is a dirty industry. But, these things happen. But we did get a Grammy nomination and it was fun because it went on. I just— and I say "I" because it's mine—but we just made a deal in Nashville. You've heard the record; the sound is not good. So we're going to bring it back up to date in about a year. Yeah, I'm pleased.

Edim: [claps] That is great! I was just going to say you should do a reunion with Benny and bring it back and do a tour. We would be there. You could sell out those fifteen hundred seats in a heartbeat.

Giovanni: No. No, I'm done. And again you have to know when to quit. That's why I was saying Vice President Harris should know not to run for president. You have to know when to quit. I'm very proud of those. I did, I think, like three albums,[28] and all three of those will be out.

You know, you just do the best you can. I think it helped to bring another concept of music and poetry, which is one of the reasons that people will say, "Well, Nikki, you're the mother of rap." At my age, I'm the grandmother. But I was one of the first people to put those things together and people began to see that we could do something different and something new. I don't know what's coming, but I hope I'm around long enough to see it. I've been watching how people are growing in music. Ice Cube and them are just about ruining rap, but there's another step coming. Black music has always kept up with the dreams of Black people. And the rest

---

[28] *Truth Is on Its Way* (1970), *Like a Ripple on a Pond* (1973), *The Way I Feel* (1975)

Ego Tripping (there may be a reason why)

I was born in the congo
I walked to the fertile crescent and built
        the sphinx
I designed a pyramid so tough that a star
        that only glows every one hundred years falls
        into the center giving divine perfect light
I am bad
I sat on the throne
        drinking nectar with allah
I got hot and sent an ice age to europe
        to cool my thirst
My oldest daughter is nefertiti
        the tears from my birth pains
        created the nile
I am a beautiful woman
I gazed on the forest and burned
        out the sahara desert
        with a packet of goat's meat
        and a change of clothes
I crossed it in two hours
I am a gazelle so swift
        so swift you can't catch me
        For a birthday present when he was three
I gave my son hannibal an elephant
        He gave me rome for mother's day
My strength flows ever on

My son noah built new/ark and
I stood proudly at the helm
        as we sailed on a soft summer day
I turned myself into myself and was
        jesus
        men intone my loving name
        All praises All praises
I am the one who would save
I sowed diamonds in my back yard
My bowels deliver uranium
        the filings from my fingernails are
        semi-precious jewels
        On a trip north
I caught a cold and blew
My nose giving oil to the arab world
I am so hip even my errors are correct
I sailed west to reach east and had to round off
        the earth as I went
        The hair from my head thinned and gold was laid
        across three continents
I am so perfect so divine so ethereal so surreal
I cannot be comprehended
        except by my permission
I mean . . . I . . . can fly
        like a bird in the sky . . .

Copyright © 1968 by Nikki Giovanni. Used with permission of the author.

of the planet has followed us. So it's going to be interesting watching it step up and to see what's coming next.

Edim: That's amazing. Thank you so much for that. We have so many questions so I'm gonna try to zoom through these. What advice do you have for poets who aspire to write their first poetry book but don't know where to start?

Giovanni: Relax. Relax and remember that you don't write every day. Nobody does and nobody should. But you need to *read* something every day. Even comics. It doesn't matter what; you should read something every day just to keep your mind going. And now we're back to pressure—we were talking about pressure—don't put pressure on yourself. Keep your eyes on the prize and there are things that you see and wonder about.

I live on a mountain and I was going down and there was a little chipmunk—and I say "she," but how would I know if it's a she—but I was thinking it's a mother and I was thinking she is taking some food down to the babies because the weather has been so weird that we have animals and mammals birthing things that they shouldn't be this time of year. So I go down the mountain at about five miles an hour—any faster, if a little chipmunk or something ran out, I would have to hit it; I wouldn't see it in time. And so I go down really slow—I can't go much slower than 5 miles an hour—and I keep my eye out on both sides just to make sure that Mrs. Chipmunk gets to her babies. You know, there are things to look at. I do write sometimes about chipmunks and somebody might think, well, that's unimportant. It probably is, but there are things to write about that you're probably thinking, well, that's not important.

You know, you have to remember, what did your grandmother cook? You might think, "Oh, nobody cares." My grandmother cooked grits every morning. Yeah, every morning you're going to eat grits. I lived with Grandmother and Grandpapa. My grandmother was quite something. She said, "My family always has two choices." That was a joke, of course, because you were supposed to say, "What's that, grandmother?" She'd say, "Take it or leave it." You learn these things. That's your choice: take it or leave it. But we knew you take it and you tell her how good it is. Unless you're a fool, and I'm a lot of things, but I'm no fool.

So that's what you do. You have to pay attention to what you're seeing and who you're seeing, responding to, or relating to. If you're in New York, then you're probably on a subway at some point and you're seeing people there and you have to be wondering, who is that? Who is that man? Is he a veteran? He's there sitting in a subway. He obviously doesn't have any place to live. The subway is home. I mean, there are questions if you pay attention. You ask for a poem? You're surrounded by poems. You just have to pay attention and respect what you're seeing.

Edim: Thank you. The next question says, "You mentioned that writers should not be afraid to contradict themselves. What advice would you have for writers in pursuit of doing this?

Giovanni: I would say, go on. The first book you write is going to be your first book, your second book is going to be your second. But you're going to eventually get to your tenth book and you don't want to look at your tenth book and say, "Oh, I said something different in my first book." That's what I'm trying to say. Don't read your first book and say I cannot say this now since I said that. Just continue with your own growth and what you're looking at, what you're seeing. Let yourself grow.

Edim: I love that. Thank you. We were talking so much about food, it looks like folks [in the online chat] want you to make a cookbook, too, if you want to add another project. So you got an album coming out. We could also do some Giovanni recipes.

Giovanni: [Laughing] That would be kind of fun. For those of us who are in New York, there's a restaurant called the Red Rooster. It's Marcus Samuelsson's and he's going to be the editor of *Bon Appétit* and *Bon Appétit* has never had a poet, and so Marcus called and asked, "Would you write a poem for me? Since I'm the editor, I'm going to do that." I told him I'd be thrilled, and I am. I wrote the poem for Marcus and I think it's the Christmas issue[29] that's coming out. I'm excited about that.

Edim: That's awesome. One of our dear editors that we love, Dawn Davis,[30] is now at *Bon Appétit,* too. I hope your worlds overlap and we get some more recipes from you. I want some lamb from Nikki.

I'm going to read a couple more questions before we end. It says here, "You are always so current with your writing. Where do you find your inspiration?"

Giovanni: I think being alive is a good idea.

But, let me go back for two seconds. I've known Dawn Davis for the longest time. She worked for my first editor, Phil Petrie. So I've known her forever. I used to tease Maya [Angelou], who was a friend, and say, "Who's writing these cookbooks for you?" And she'd say, "I am!" I said, "Oh, you can't cook." We would argue about who can cook and who can't. So I'm kind of scared [of publishing recipes]. But maybe at some point.

Toni Morrison, who didn't really cook that much either, really liked porgies, the fish. And so every time I was in New York I'd go to Chelsea

---

[29] "3-1593 400 Mulvaney Street" appeared in the December 2020 issue of *Bon Appétit*.

[30] Dawn Davis (1965 -) is a publisher, author, and editor. In November 2020 she became the first Black editor of *Bon Appétit*.

Market and I'd get a couple of porgies, or, actually, even more, and I'd call her. She lived up on the Hudson and I would fry the fish for her. Frying fish is difficult. The trick is slow, you cook it slowly. And ginger makes everything better. I use ginger a lot. I use it for my chicken. You know, you're frying something and you throw a little ginger in there and everybody will say, what is that?

Edim: I usually put garlic in everything, but I'm going to try the ginger trick.

Giovanni: You'll love it.

Edim: Our next question is, "How do I continue to encourage my students to build and believe in the power of their voices and make time for their writing while doing that?

Giovanni: I think the main thing is—and I do it with my students—you want to find something that they've written that is good, so you can say, "Oh, that's really nice." Whether it's, "I really liked where you put that word," or, "Golly, I would have thought that that line would have gone there and you put it there. That was really cool." You want to find a way to praise because eventually you're going to be gone and they're going to be twenty years old and in college or something and you want them used to hearing praise. And that's what you're going to do. And as you encourage them to look at what they're writing, because the words are important, but the placement of the words is also important. And so what you want to do is, "Oh look, I just couldn't believe it when I saw that you did that." And the kid is going to be happy. They'll continue to find the time to do it.

We forget all the time that athletes—particularly basketball players—they keep going out and they keep shooting the basketball and shooting the basketball and they miss many more times than they actually get it. But they keep doing it and they get to the point where they can shoot that basketball more.

Edim: Yes. It's a practice.

Giovanni: Practice and praise. You also get praise.

I teach at Virginia Tech and we're a football power, and I like football anyway, but having watched Colin Kaepernick, having watched him kneel, that was just a beautiful thing. And as I was talking to the football team—they invited me over—I said, "You know, this is what I know as a woman: men kneel when they are going to ask a woman, will you be mine?" That's what they do. If Colin kneels in front of the flag, he's saying to America, "Will you be mine?" No matter what anybody else says, he is asking America to be mine. And it's up to America to say yes. Right now, under Donald Trump, we've been hearing no. So under Biden and Kamala we might hear—he's on his knees saying would you be mine and the answer should be, "Yes, I'll be yours."

Edim: Yes. You mentioned Virginia Tech and I'm from Northern Virginia. I had a lot of friends that went to Virginia Tech and they took your classes. I was always so jealous—you took a class with Nikki Giovanni?! There's a question here that says, "Can you tell the story of Virginia Tech and how you came to be there?" You've been there almost two decades. You could have your pick of schools. So how did you make your way to the small Blacksburg, Virginia?

Giovanni: I was recruited and it was one of those things where you just felt comfortable. I am, as I said earlier, an Appalachian. I'm from Knoxville. And I'm not against, you know, Harvard or something, but you start to do that and that takes over. I wanted to be someplace that I was comfortable. Virginia Fowler recruited me and I thought, "Well, that'll work." I asked my mother—my father had died and I was living with Mommy—I wrote a poem, you know, "I Married My Mother"[31]—and I said to Mommy, "You want to move to Virginia?" And she said, "I'll go wherever. I'm going with you." I used to tease her about that. I said, "You should have married me." So we moved here and we've been here.

But the funniest thing that I can share…as an artist you get paid first—and I'm sorry Aretha is not here, she can tell you about that—and then you go on stage. When I took the job and I got a paycheck, I thought, "Well, that's really nice." You know, you see a paycheck, you go and put it in the bank. And then, about two weeks later, I got another paycheck and I said to Ginney, "I don't know what to do. There's been a mistake. They already paid me and this is another check." She said, "Oh no, you get two checks a month," and I said, "Damn, had I known that I would have taken a job a long time ago."

Edim: I love that. We're going to take two more questions from the question box before we have to leave you. What is a piece of your own writing that got across exactly what you wanted to express or shifted your creative trajectory?

Giovanni: I think probably "Ego Tripping" would be the poem that did exactly what I wanted it to do because you're always being asked, "Who are you?" Now, in the old days, if I had been born in slavery, the old women would have said, if anybody asks you who are, tell them you're a child of God. You must know that song, and that's a good song. But as I came up, if anybody asks who I was I'm going to say, "I was created. I was born in the Congo. I created this Earth. I'm the one who made

---

[31] "I Married My Mother" appears in *A Good Cry: What We Learn From Tears and Laughter* (William Morrow, 2017).

it." That's what "Ego Tripping" did. And I was so pleased because, you know, you write a poem and you don't know—I can say that to all the writers out there—you don't know how it's going to be received. And nor do you care. You're just going to write the best one that you can. I was so pleased that people saw "Ego Tripping" the way that I saw it, that Earth was created by Black women because there's nothing that's more important than Black women. It's true. And I don't see how Black women can wake up in the morning and not just say to themselves, "God, I'm wonderful." You know, just when you go look in the mirror to brush your teeth you just have to smile at yourself. It may be the only smile you get that day because people are fools, but you have to know, I'm wonderful. I'm wonderful. And that's a good thing.

I've written a poem that's in this book, *Make Me Rain*. "What a shame that white boys wake up in the morning and all they have to offer is the color of their skin."[32] What a shame. That would be embarrassing if all I had to offer was the color of my skin. Because Black women have everything to offer. We cook. We clean. We do everything. We're loving. We're funny. We do everything.

Edim: We do.

Giovanni: We do. We do.

---

[32] The only thing you have to offer
Anything...yourself...Planet Earth
Anything at all.
Is
Your white skin

How sad. How sad.

From "And So It Comes to This," *Make Me Rain* (2020)

Edim: Wow. This has just been so amazing. I feel so blessed. I'm so thankful for you. Everyone, buy this book [*Make Me Rain*], continue to buy this book.

Are you on Twitter or Instagram or anything?

Giovanni: [Sighs] I think so. I think my publishers—what is that thing called? Facebook?[33] Yeah, they have that. I just don't do that. You know, you have to be careful when you're talking to strangers. And I say that to my students. They get on that thing and they tweet. I look at Donald Trump. He's always tweeting. Who the hell do you think you're talking to? You have to be careful. You don't want to spend your time talking to people you don't know who are lying to you. Because they always lie. "Oh, I had a great time last night. Oh, I had this." And they didn't have diddly-squat. If you had all of that, where did you get the time to write to me?

Edim: I do want to sneak in one last question from one of our favorite poets, Khadijah Queen[34]. What is one aspect of your vision for the future of literature?

Giovanni: Well, literature—words—will always be with us and I think words are winning now. There was a time—well, just look at the history. I'm a Christian so I look at Jesus because it's easy. You're going to crucify somebody because you don't like the words that he's saying and we've brought that idea along [into the present]. I think words will continue to be incredibly important, and one of the reasons that I was so

---

[33] Nikki Giovanni's Facebook page is www.facebook.com/NikkiGiovanniAuthor

[34] Khadijah Queen, PhD, is the author of six books, including *I'm So Fine: A List of Famous Men & What I Had On* (YesYes Books, 2017).

proud—you all sent me a t-shirt[35], by the way, "Well-Read Black Girl." I have a fourteen-year-old granddaughter and I think there's just probably nothing in the world better than daughters. I have a son and I love him. I think he's a great kid, I really do, but he had enough sense to give me a granddaughter. And so I sent it to her so that she can wear "Well-Read Black Girl."

Edim: I love that. If she ever wants to come to the community, come to a book club, we are more than happy to welcome her.

And thank you so much for everything you've done for Black women, for continuing to have a vision and leading us into a new era of open-mindedness. I feel like your words also bring us such peace and like there's a space where I can know what my interior self is when I read your work. I know that you are writing and loving me unconditionally. So just thank you for loving us and being with the Well-Read Black Girl community. Thank you so much.

Giovanni: Well, thank you. I'm delighted and call on me anytime. If I can be of any service you let me know.

---

[35] You can purchase Well-Read Black Girl t-shirts and sweatshirts at www.wellreadblackgirl.com